THE HEYDAY OF
TYSELEY
AND ITS
LOCOMOTIVES

MICHAEL WHITEHOUSE
and
IAN HOGARTH

Ian Allan
PUBLISHING

First published 2003

ISBN 0 7110 2926 1

Published by Ian Allan Publishing

an imprint of Ian Allan Publishing Ltd, Hersham, Surrey KT12 4RG.
Printed by Ian Allan Printing Ltd, Hersham, Surrey KT12 4RG.

Code: 0302/B

Introduction

The word 'heyday' commonly conjures up visions of the dim and distant past, but not at Tyseley. The depot now has more famous engines either based there or as visitors than ever before. Hopefully in the future it will have more still; that, certainly, is the intention, as both the depot and the vintage trains which run from it gain increasing national and international reputations.

There has been steam at Tyseley continuously since 1908. The depot was built on a greenfield site to cater for the growth in traffic on the GWR in the Birmingham area with the development of city suburban services, the opening of the new cross-country route through Stratford and Cheltenham to the west and the growth of freight traffic, not least the Moor Street fruit market near the Bull Ring.

Tyseley was constructed in standard GWR modular buildings: two roundhouses (one for passenger engines, the other for freight), a coal stage with electric lifting platform for coal tubs and a factory for repairs. Provision was made for two further roundhouses but these were never constructed, engines being stored outside near the Warwick Road frontage and easily visible from the top of a bus, their brass and copperwork glinting in the summer sunshine; *Lady of Lynne*, *Saint Helena*, *Ivanhoe*, *Rob Roy*, several 'Halls' and a whole host of pannier tanks and eight-coupled goods engines could be seen. It was not easy for the casual visitor to gain access to the shed, but if one was bold and ventured into the Stygian interior of the roundhouses, one was rewarded with an awesome feast of engines gathered round two turntables, some with their features picked out by the shafts of sunlight penetrating through the windows in the roof.

Tyseley's motive power remained more or less unchanged through the years, although more modern engines gradually replaced the Dean, then Churchward and Collett designs. Tyseley was never a top-link shed, but during the late 1950s and early 1960s it became host to an extraordinary series of unusual or elite engines for enthusiast specials — the inspiration of Arthur Camwell of the Stephenson Locomotive Society. *Skylark*, *Saint David*, *Princess Margaret*, *King Henry VI* and *County of Chester* all took their turn on trains, usually to Swindon, having been groomed at Tyseley the week before, with the front number being painted on the buffer-beam in true GWR tradition in a last defiant gesture to the nationalised railway.

Tyseley did not escape the effects of the Modernisation Plan, the fleet of 2-6-2Ts giving way to diesel multiple-units in the

Right: Tyseley shed was opened by the Great Western Railway in 1908 to provide stabling, servicing and repair facilities for its locomotives in the West Midlands. The shed featured two roundhouses (one passenger, one freight) as well as a heavy-repair shop, coaling stage and watering and ashpit disposal facilities. Now it is home to a collection of preserved locomotives and occasionally features visitors at galas. Here on 17 September 1988 the sun rises over a catholic collection of LMS-group locomotives assembled for London & Birmingham 150, including *Cornwall*, *Kolhapur*, *Princess Elizabeth* and *Rocket*. *Michael Whitehouse*

1960s. But, elated with special-train fever, the shed proved a magnet to small GWR tank engines which had been preserved. Nos 4555, 6435 and 1638 were all to be found in the roundhouse on their way to the Dart Valley Railway purchased by Midlands businessmen Pat Whitehouse and Pat Garland. Shedmaster Tommy Field — a man prepared to make decisions and stand by them — saw no reason why 4555 should not be used, even though it was not the property of his lords and masters. Thus, to the delight of the commuters, daily routine would sometimes be shattered by a sparkling green 'Small Prairie' on the 5.05pm Snow Hill all-stations to Knowle & Dorridge. The heyday had begun.

Running these trains was fun. It was easy for the two Pats to pop down to the shed after Sunday lunch to see their engines and

Above: It's the last day of Tyseley steam shed. A brazier is still alight, but the last fires in the steam engines have been dropped. No 9630 stands outside, destined for the scrapyard, as a Brush Type 4 diesel waits for tomorrow, on 31 December 1966. *Michael Whitehouse*

Below: A rare sight indeed. GWR railcar No 2 stands outside Tyseley 'factory' when new during the 1930s. The railcars were introduced to provide a fast service on the route from Birmingham to Cardiff. *Arthur Flowers (Millbrook House Collection)*

Right: The sunlight invades the sulphurous gloom of Tyseley roundhouse, illuminating a Robinson ROD 2-8-0 adapted by the GWR and numbered 3012. On the right are GWR '28xx' No 2856 and 'Modified Hall' No 7913 *Little Wyrley Hall*. *Pat Whitehouse*

drink tea with Tommy. So, when *Clun Castle* was bought for preservation, it seemed a pity to take it to Buckfastleigh as originally intended. Many societies wanted to hire it to run trains, so it came to Tyseley instead; diesels had made big inroads, and by 1966 there was room in the shed. Pat Whitehouse often went to London for board meetings, travelling back on the 4.10pm from Paddington to Banbury. There he would detrain and walk over to the depot where *Clun Castle* had been sent to meet him, and together they would come back on the 'carflat' empties for Washwood Heath — a private express engine on a BR freight working, all for the owner's enjoyment.

It couldn't last, of course. In 1966 the shed closed to steam. On the last day of the year the only sign of life was the burning embers from a brazier, casting flickering shadows on a silent pannier standing forlorn near the shed doorway. Outside stood a Brush Type 4 diesel, patiently waiting for tomorrow.

Above left: Pannier tanks are still shedded at Tyseley. Great Western Railway 0-6-0PT No 7760 stands on the demonstration line at Tyseley with a GWR shunter's truck one night in 2001. *Derek Huntriss*

Left: Continuing the tradition of 'Halls' being the main type of named engine at Tyseley, No 4936 *Kinlet Hall* stands alongside Tyseley Warwick Road signalbox in 2001, awaiting its next duties. *Derek Huntriss*

Far right: 'Return to Tyseley', painted on the side of a GWR 'Fruit D' wagon. Make sure you do, soon. *Michael Whitehouse*

But Tyseley 'Loco' never did die. *Clun Castle* remained and was joined by 'foreigner' *Kolhapur*, an LMS 'Jubilee' from Leeds. Together they were stored and repainted in the converted coaling stage as the roundhouse was knocked down and the vestiges of the steam age swept away.

The men of Tyseley hung on. Pat Whitehouse and Chief Engineer Jim Kent prepared for a siege but also for the future, laying the groundwork for heydays to come. Whilst the two 4-6-0s were imprisoned during the BR steam ban from 1968 to 1972 the Tyseley team scoured the depots and works at Leamington, Gloucester and Worcester for tools and spares; they built up an enviable machine-shop capacity, installing wheel-lathe and wheel-drop, and a new shed to house more engines, including several from the National Collection whilst the new museum at York was being constructed. Thus *Sir Lamiel*, *Cheltenham*, the LSWR 'T9' 4-4-0 and the LYR 2-4-2T came to Tyseley on exhibition and, together with the resident locomotives, formed the centrepieces for some highly successful open days.

Starved of main-line steam, enthusiasts and Birmingham locals flocked to Tyseley once or twice a year to see the giants of steam pace up and down on a caged site. Mouth-watering visitors such as such as *Flying Scotsman*, *King George V* and *Princess Elizabeth* ran around to thrill sometimes over 18,000 people in one day, and all for 7s 6d. Sometimes the resident fleet would escape to open days in London or Liverpool, nominally hauled by a diesel, but when officialdom was out of sight the diesel would shut down and 'Clun' and *Kolhapur* would take turns at thrashing down the main line. Steam at Tyseley wasn't going to die.

In June 1972 BR finally relented and allowed limited steam runs to resume. *Clun Castle* was first off and left Bordesley in the pouring rain for Didcot. Even pannier No 7752 was occasionally allowed out on some shuttles to Stratford, mischievously taking a GWR 'Fruit D' van full of coal to lay over at Moor Street station as part of the consist!

In the 1980s the depot was opened more to the public, with a startling array of visiting engines attending open days and celebrations, notably the 150th anniversaries of the GWR and the London & Birmingham Railway. The shed had never seen such glamorous and idiosyncratic machines: *Rocket*, *Lion*, *Cornwall*, *King Edward I*, North London 0-6-0T No 76, Brighton 'Terrier' *Sutton*, a vertical-boiled Sentinel, the Courtaulds 'Flying Bufferbeam' Peckett 0-4-0T, Taff Vale 0-6-2T No 28, 'B1' *Mayflower*, 'A4' *Sir Nigel Gresley*, 'V2' *Green Arrow* — the list is almost endless.

The Tyseley team had always thought that the future of main-line steam would be on short-haul trips to places of interest, allowing time for passengers to look around at the destination. BR fought against this concept, but Tyseley won the day with the inaugural weekend of eight 'Shakespeare Express' trains from Birmingham to Stratford in 1985. Carrying 3,000 people in a weekend and serving breakfast, lunch and dinner in GWR saloons, the trains were a resounding success. But it was not until the privatisation of the railways that Tyseley engines were able to blossom on the main line. The current team carefully assessed the risks and opportunities of the new era from their strong position of knowledge of the new system, and in 1999 the 'Shakespeare Express' was launched as a regular summer-timetabled train, gaining instant appeal and catapulting Tyseley into the top league of main-line steam operators.

The engineering side of the operation was developed too: given the name Tyseley Locomotive Works, it began to undertake serious overhauls on steam engines for individuals and heritage railways. *Defiant* and *Rood Ashton Hall* were reconstructed from scrapyard wrecks, panniers 7760 and 9600 were outshopped for scampering round local lines, and attention is currently being given to the overhaul of a fleet of coaches fit for the 21st century, to be hauled by express steam engines under the Vintage Trains banner.

Having saved a collection of locomotives, machinery and spare parts from the scrapheap and turned it into something useful again by preserving, teaching and using the skills of the steam age, the Tyseley team have fulfilled their initial ambitions of keeping steam in trust for the future as an educational charity. The task now is to perpetuate the heyday by ensuring the vision can be maintained — to continue to operate steam trains on the main line (as they used to be) but on the modern railway and in the 21st century. Hopefully the best is yet to come!

Michael Whitehouse
Ian Hogarth
October 2002

Left: A summer Sunday, 29 July 1962, and 1950-built No 7029 *Clun Castle* takes water at Lapworth troughs while hauling the 1.10pm Paddington–Wolverhampton Low Level service, before any thought of the Ian Allan 1964 swansong trains which were to set the scene for preservation. *Michael Mensing*

Above: GWR Prairie No 4555 was rescued by preservationists Pat Whitehouse and Pat Garland to run on the Dart Valley Railway and arrived at Tyseley in 1964 for a repaint, which was undertaken in the old factory. No 4555 was then used on BR revenue-earning trains, including the 5.05 Snow Hill–Knowle & Dorridge, courtesy of Tommy Field, the shedmaster, before moving to Worcester and then Buckfastleigh. Notice the new diesel depot under construction in the background. *Pat Whitehouse*

Below: An interesting combination on 17 October 1965 as GWR 0-6-0PT No 6435 (with Pat Whitehouse on the footplate) pilots 'Castle' No 7029 *Clun Castle* past Wick Bridge, between Berkeley Road and Charfield, on an SLS special from Birmingham to Bristol. No 6435 had been repainted at Tyseley by B. Whitehouse & Sons, the Whitehouse family building firm, and was *en route* to the Dart Valley Railway to start a new life in Devon. *Hugh Ballantyne*

Right: GWR 'Grange' locomotives had a reputation as being fine engines, and Tyseley was fortunate to have examples. On 21 November 1965 No 6861 *Crynant Grange* stands outside Tyseley shed. *Neville Simms*

Below right: A type that was commonly allocated to Tyseley was the GWR 2-6-0 (Mogul). Here No 5369 stands on the ashpits and servicing roads leading to the roundhouse. In the background can be seen the carriage shed, some suburban stock, and a cafeteria car. The date is 26 November 1961. *Neville Simms*

Above: In later years Tyseley became home to various types of engine from the London Midland Region, as the shed moved into the LMR as of 1966. On 21 November 1965 ex-LMS 2-6-0 No 46470 is seen out of steam at Tyseley, sandwiched between two 'Black Fives', the rear engine being No 45134. *Neville Simms*

Right: By 22 November 1964 the GWR allocation at Tyseley was dwindling. Here, GWR 'Grange' 4-6-0 No 6853 *Morehampton Grange*, a long-term Tyseley resident, sits alongside 'Castle' No 5014 *Goodrich Castle* and 'Modified Hall' No 7918 *Rhose Wood Hall*. Intriguingly, No 6853 nearly made it into preservation; Pat Whitehouse declined to buy it for £1,200 when it was found to have a cracked steam manifold. We have kicked ourselves ever since! *Neville Simms*

Left: Tyseley was home to several GWR 2-8-0 '28xx' heavy-freight engines. Here No 2856 approaches Madeley Junction signalbox, east of Wellington, on the Wolverhampton–Shrewsbury line, plodding steadily uphill with a down freight. The date is 27 August 1962. *Michael Mensing*

Above: Doing what the class did best — hauling a suburban train — GWR Large Prairie No 4110, a Tyseley resident, leaves Soho & Winson Green on 25 November 1961 with the 1.45pm Stourbridge Junction–Birmingham Snow Hill. *Michael Mensing*

15

Left: A locomotive that was allocated to Tyseley for most of its life was GWR Large Prairie No 8109, seen here in Snow Hill station's Platform 12 with a six-coach train on 16 April 1963. The engine is in good condition externally for such a late date and sports Tyseley's 84E shedplate. Tyseley was home to many such locomotives. *Neville Simms*

Above: The new era sweeps in as a three-car WR suburban DMU (later Class 116) waits to leave Birmingham Snow Hill's Platform 7 with the 1.05pm to Stratford-upon-Avon. The date is 9 June 1962 and the service is a Saturdays-only, calling at Henley-in-Arden. Tyseley was one of the first depots to be home to the new multiple-units and to this day services DMUs for the Midlands and beyond. *Michael Mensing*

Left: It is 27 September 1964, and GWR 'County' No 1011 *County of Chester*, having arrived at Swindon, stands outside the works with a Stephenson Locomotive Society special from Birmingham. No 1011 was prepared at Tyseley and, in the tradition of such special trains, had its GWR-style front number repainted on the front buffer-beam. Arthur Camwell, Secretary of the SLS Midlands Area and Editor of the Society's journal, organised many trains from Birmingham to Swindon for the last member of each class, including 'Bulldog' No 3454 *Skylark*, 'Star' No 4056 *Princess Margaret*, No 6018 *King Henry VI* and No 4079 *Pendennis Castle*. All the engines were prepared at Tyseley, and so the seeds were sown for the preservation team. *J. R. Reed*

Right: During the 1960s a new Hegenscheidt wheel-lathe was installed in Tyseley diesel depot which could turn wheels *in situ*, without the need for a wheel-drop. A procession of steam engines duly visited Tyseley to have their wheels corrected; here Stanier 2-6-4T No 42069 receives attention in May 1966. Although this wheel-lathe is now out of commission, it is part of the National Collection, and will be installed in the next phase of development at Tyseley Locomotive Works. *Steve Hewins*

Above: An unidentified Standard Class 4 2-6-0 (a type which visited Tyseley infrequently) moves forward from the roundhouse for water alongside an LMS 'Mickey Mouse' 2-6-0 during the 1960s. *Steve Hewins*

Left: Pannier tanks and Tyseley are synonymous, both in steam days and in preservation. Here No 9774 stands on the coaling road by the water column in a classic early-evening shot during May 1966. *Steve Hewins*

Right: The end of steam is near as ex-LMS engines dominate the scene at Tyseley. From left to right are '8F' No 48061 and 'Black Fives' Nos 44859 and 44774. *Steve Hewins*

Above: No 7029 *Clun Castle* gained fame by heading the Western Region 'Farewell to Steam' railtour from Paddington to Bristol on 27 November 1965. The train is seen near Chippenham. *Tony Bowles*

Above: From time to time, *Clun Castle* would be steamed in the shed yard at Tyseley for the owners' enjoyment on a Sunday afternoon. Here it stands at the top of the yard in authentic ex-BR unkempt condition, with future Chairman Michael Whitehouse driving on a break from school. Who said driving courses are a new invention? *Pat Whitehouse*

Above: No 7029 *Clun Castle* stands inside the Tyseley passenger roundhouse, posing for artist Terence Cuneo, on Monday 6 March 1967 — the day after it had hauled the last train from Birkenhead to Birmingham Snow Hill, bringing down the final curtain on main-line steam at Snow Hill. The steam shed had already closed at the end of the previous year, but preservation activities had just begun. *Pat Whitehouse*

Right: On 4 March 1967 No 7029 stands under the GWR coaling stage at Tyseley, being prepared for the weekend of trains to Birkenhead — the end of BR express steam in Birmingham, but the beginning of its re-creation in preservation. *Pat Whitehouse*

Left: Looking absolutely splendid (albeit with incorrect red frames), GWR 'Castle' class 4-6-0 No 4079 *Pendennis Castle* stands at the shed exit signal in the yard at Tyseley after the SLS last runs to Birkenhead in March 1967.
Ken Cooper(Michael Whitehouse Collection)

Above: The darkness of the roundhouse and the contrasting lights overhead illuminate the first stages of preservation. Nos 7029 *Clun Castle* and 4079 *Pendennis Castle* and ex-LNER 'K4' No 3442 *The Great Marquess* rest in the roundhouse on 8 March 1967, all being present to feature in various Cuneo paintings. Outside can be seen a snowplough, with the lights of the houses on the Warwick Road behind. *Neville Simms*

Left: Rescued by Brian Hollingsworth and Eric Drury, ex-LMS 'Black Five' 4-6-0 No 45428, later to be named *Eric Treacy*, was an early preservation resident of Tyseley. It is seen here immediately after arrival under its own steam from Holbeck shed in Leeds, taking water outside the old roundhouse. Bernard Rainbow, Tyseley driver and first Depot Superintendent in the preservation era, is at the water crane. The date is 24 August 1968 — just after the end of steam. *Michael Whitehouse*

Above: It is 31 October 1970, and No 4983 *Albert Hall* (later discovered to be No 4965 *Rood Ashton Hall*) is seen immediately after arrival from Barry scrapyard after purchase. The tenth engine to leave the yard for preservation, it was hauled to Tyseley at 50mph, still with connecting rods fitted and with Jim Kent, Tyseley's Chief Engineer, on the footplate. *Michael Whitehouse*

Left: Heading the test train prior to the lifting of the steam ban, GWR 'King' No 6000 *King George V* enters Tyseley station with a train from Hereford on 1 October 1971. The success of this run allowed engines such as No 7029 *Clun Castle* back onto the main line. *Michael Whitehouse*

Right: During the BR steam ban, main-line engines were limited to depot yards. The Tyseley team took advantage of this and sponsored open days jointly with BR. Here GWR 'King' No 6000 *King George V* is seen on the shuttle train on the goods loop (with ex-LMS 4-6-2 No 6201 *Princess Elizabeth* at the other end) amongst an amazing 18,000 visitors on 2 October 1971. *Michael Whitehouse*

Below: Princess Elizabeth runs shuttle trains with *King George V* on the Tyseley goods loop on 3 October with the infamous 'tin-pan alley' of society stalls in the dustbowl in the foreground. *Michael Whitehouse*

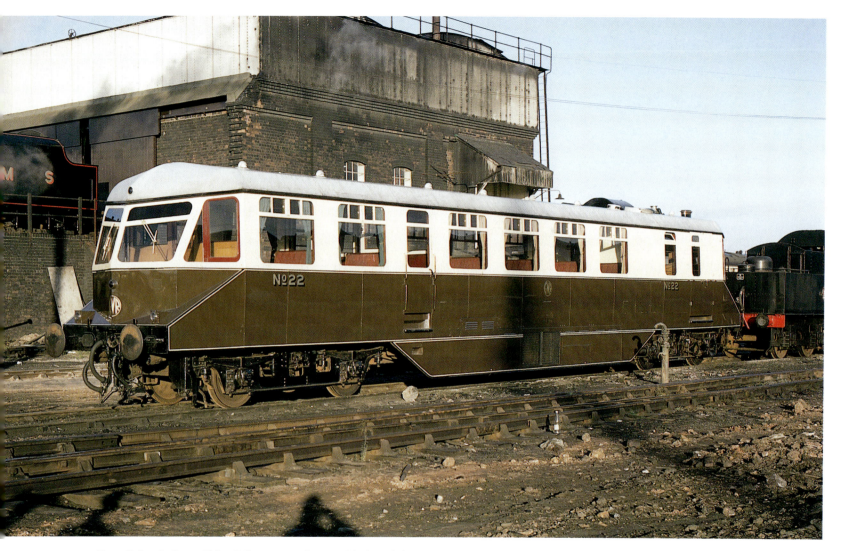

Above: Before the Severn Valley Railway reopened, many of the items in its collection came to Tyseley open days. Here GWR railcar No 22 re-creates a scene from the past — operation of the Birmingham–Cardiff express by its streamlined sisters — at an open day in May 1972. Compare this with the picture on page 4 for a contrast in periods. *Pat Whitehouse*

Right: To house Tyseley's locomotives and workshop equipment, a new charity, the Standard Gauge Steam Trust, was formed. There was initially some spare space in the workshop, and so, prior to the opening of the National Railway Museum in York, some exhibits were removed from store in Brighton so they could be seen again. Two of these were Southern Railway express engines. Here 'King Arthur' No 30777 *Sir Lamiel* and 'Schools' No 30925 *Cheltenham* stand in the shed yard (cleared for an open day), with Pullman cars *Ione* and *Ibis* (both now in the VSOE set) forming a backdrop, in May 1972. *Pat Whitehouse*

Left: Standing outside the shed at Tyseley on arrival from London Transport, No L94 is actually the former GWR No 7752! This was the last steam engine to see service with London Transport and as a result achieved fame, appearing on the front of a number of national daily newspapers. Pat Whitehouse acquired two of the last three LT panniers (Nos 7752 and 7760), with the third (5764) going to the SVR. They were well-maintained engines and came with several spare parts. No 7752 became a reliable and favourite performer at Tyseley. Taken in July 1971, this shot shows the engine in LT red prior to repainting in GWR green for excursions and depot use. *Pat Whitehouse*

Above: No 7752 stands in the carriage sidings at Tyseley with a train of empty coaching stock for Birmingham Moor Street on 13 May 1973. It was preparing to work shuttles from Birmingham to Stratford-upon-Avon, which sowed the seeds of the 'Shakespeare Express' we know today. Note the 'Fruit D' van from the Museum collection, attached to carry tools and coal! This was done without the need for any certificates or approvals — main-line running was simpler in 1973!
Michael Whitehouse

Left: Ex-LNER 'V2' 2-6-2 No 4771 *Green Arrow* was saved for the National Collection and stored at Leicester for many years before being restored to steam by Bill Harvey, the former shedmaster at Norwich. Pat Whitehouse negotiated for it to have its first main-line runs from Tyseley, and this photograph shows the locomotive immediately after arrival at Tyseley in May 1973, repainted and resplendent in LNER apple green, before running a series of shuttle trains to Stratford. Next to it is the National Railway Museum's former LSWR 'T9' 4-4-0, No 120. *Michael Whitehouse*

Above: LNER-designed 'A2' Pacific No 532 *Blue Peter* at Tyseley open day on 6 October 1974, leading the famous shuttle trains on the goods loop. This was one of the locomotive's rare appearances in apple green ahead of its main-line career in preservation. *Michael Whitehouse*

Above: In 1973 No 7029 *Clun Castle* made two return trips from Birmingham Moor Street to Warwick, sponsored by various local newspapers. Here it is on the second run of the day, accelerating through Bordesley off the viaduct after leaving Birmingham Moor Street. The empty trackbed once carrying the lines to Snow Hill can be clearly seen. *Derek Huntriss*

Right: Liverpool & Manchester Railway 0-4-2 *Lion* was preserved in Liverpool's City Museum. Michael Whitehouse got to know Adrian Jarvis, the museum's curator, as a result of the Liverpool & Manchester 150th-anniversary celebrations, and, having always admired *Lion* during university days, decided to ask if Tyseley could borrow it; the answer was 'yes'! Thus *Lion* ran at Tyseley for a week in October 1980, carrying 10,000 people in the replica Third-class L&M open coaches — a highlight of the preservation era at Tyseley. *Michael Whitehouse*

Far left: The Standard Gauge Steam Trust created workshops from scratch on the ash roads of the old depot. A new shed was built to house the former Ipswich wheel-drop and Bescot wheel-lathe and to provide machinery facilities. Ex-LMS 'Jubilee' No 5593 *Kolhapur* receives axlebox attention. *Michael Whitehouse*

Left: The year 1983 saw the 75th anniversary of the opening of Tyseley shed, and a gala was held with GWR pannier No 7752 as the star. The locomotive is seen here on 12 June, in immaculate condition and covered in flags and bunting. *Michael Whitehouse*

Below: Don Green, formerly Works Manager at Worcester, bores No 7029's valves at Tyseley Locomotive Works in 1984. *Birmingham Railway Museum Trust*

Left: In 1984, whilst *Clun Castle* and *Kolhapur* were under repair, Tyseley had no large engine to steam for demonstration-line passenger trips and so hired in LNER-designed 'B1' 4-6-0 No 1306 *Mayflower*, seen here on the shuttle at Tyseley. *Michael Whitehouse*

Above: During GW150 year (1985) Tyseley staged a large gala to celebrate the anniversary, which also featured the launch of the 'Shakespeare Express'. Several visiting engines made appearances at galas, and Taff Vale Railway 0-6-2T No 28 is shown outside the workshop being prepared for the day's events in June 1985. *Anthony J. Lambert*

Left: Clun Castle returns home in 1985 for the GW150 celebrations on 6 September 1985. No 7029 takes a Truro–Plymouth train over Coombe St Stephens Viaduct — a timeless Great Western scene. For most of its working life No 7029 was a Newton Abbot engine and frequently worked into Cornwall and South Wales. *Andrew Bell*

Above: June 1986, and 0-4-4T Metropolitan Railway No 1 features alongside a smart No 7029 *Clun Castle* in preparation for a gala. *Michael Whitehouse*

Left: Following the success of Tyseley's return to main-line steam-train operation for GW150 in 1985, the Trustees agreed to restore a third main-line engine, and grant funds were obtained from the City of Birmingham, the Borough of Sandwell and the Manpower Services Commission. With restoration about to commence, 0-6-0PT No 7760 moves derelict-looking 'Castle' No 5080 *Defiant* into the workshops on a freezing day in December 1985 for its fast-track (18-month) restoration to main-line condition. *Michael Whitehouse*

Below left: A feature of the well-equipped Tyseley Locomotive Works is the wheel-lathe, acquired from Bescot shed. No 5080's wheels are seen receiving attention in 1986. *Michael Whitehouse*

Right: No 5080 *Defiant* was withdrawn on 11 April 1963 and sold for scrap. Having been rescued from Barry scrapyard as a source of spare parts for No 7029, it was stored until 1985. After a whirlwind restoration, it was steamed for the first time on 16 July 1987, all those who helped being pictured alongside. This was a fantastic day, and, for the first time in many years, Tyseley had two working 'Castles'. *Michael Whitehouse*

Left: A 'Castle' on the main line: after its 18-month rebuild, No 5080 *Defiant* hauls a Didcot–Tyseley train up Hatton Bank on 11 June 1988 on its return to the main line — a faultless performance. No 5080 saw limited use on the main line but toured other preserved railways, including the Gloucestershire–Warwickshire Railway, the East Lancs Railway and the Llangollen Railway. *Defiant* was also the star of the Drive-a-Loco courses for the general public, which were a huge success at Tyseley and led to many enthusiasts' experiencing the footplate. *Andrew Bell*

Above: It's a sunny 8 August 1988, and many admirers watch a beautifully turned out No 5080 *Defiant* run through Cheltenham Spa on the 'Red Dragon' towards Newport. Behind the engine is the support coach, 17018, with 'Birmingham Railway Museum' on the roof. *Defiant* was withdrawn from service in 1997 and in 2002 went on display at the Buckinghamshire Railway Centre, Quainton. *Malcolm Ranieri*

Above: October 1985, and ex-LMS 'Duchess' 4-6-2 No 46229 *Duchess of Hamilton* pauses at Tyseley for water whilst working a special train. The opportunity was taken to line up No 46229 with Tyseley resident No 5593 *Kolhapur* and fellow 'Jubilee' No 5690 *Leander*, which had arrived from the Severn Valley Railway for repairs requiring access to the wheel-drop. *Michael Whitehouse*

Left : No 5593 *Kolhapur* is seen here at Manchester Victoria in September 1986 whilst running a series of day excursions to Southport. *Michael Whitehouse*

Right: Having returned to the main line in GW150 year, No 5593 was in demand as a 'new' engine for railtours. Birmingham Railway Museum organised some of its own, including a trip each way on the Settle–Carlisle line, its stamping-ground immediately prior to withdrawal in 1967. The locomotive is pictured approaching Smardale on 21 March 1987. *Malcolm Ranieri*

Above: On 25 April 1987 No 5593 *Kolhapur* is seen on home territory at Peak Forest Junction Tunnel with a Buxton–Derby train — a route not commonly used by charter trains. The noise of the exhaust reverberating off the rockface has to be imagined! *Andrew Bell*

Right: On 27 March 1988 No 5593 *Kolhapur* visited the Severn Valley Railway. Partnered with LNER teak coaches, it is seen at Hay Bridge with the 4.45pm from Kidderminster Town to Bridgnorth. *Andrew Bell*

Above: In September 1988 the opportunity was taken to line up the working Great Western locomotives of the Tyseley collection during the London & Birmingham 150 celebrations. From left to right are No 7029 *Clun Castle*, 0-6-0PT No 7752, No 5080 *Defiant* and newly restored 0-6-0PT No 7760. *Michael Whitehouse*

Right: Tyseley's pannier No 7760 crosses Dee Bridge on the Llangollen Railway with the 2.45pm from Llangollen on 28 August 1989. Like No 7752, No 7760 has toured many preserved railways but in 1997 was outshopped from Tyseley Locomotive Works as main-line-approved and has found a new lease of life operating in tandem with fellow pannier tank No 9600 to a variety of destinations across the Midlands on day excursions and evening trains. *Andrew Bell*

Left: No 7760 gallops past Swithland sidings with a Rothley–Leicester North service on the Great Central Railway with a push-pull train used when this section of the line was first open to the public after reconstruction. *Malcolm Ranieri*

Above : No 5593 *Kolhapur* with the GCR's dining train, running past Swithland on the Great Central Railway on 3 March 1991. At this time the GCR had three Tysesley engines (Nos 7029, 5593 and 7760 on loan together with GWR special saloon No 9001, all of which helped start the GCR's 'big engine' policy and its revival in recreating the double-track main-line image. *Andrew Bell*

Left: Pannier No 7752 was built in 1930 by the North British Locomotive Co in Glasgow. It has seen many years of service on loan to an impressive list of preserved railways, being pictured here at Winchcombe on the Gloucestershire Warwickshire Railway with the 2pm train from Toddington on 30 March 1991. No 7752 has visited this railway twice, and for a while was partnered with fellow Tyseley resident No 5080 *Defiant. Andrew Bell*

Above: Boxing Day 1991, with the sun setting over Leicestershire and GWR pannier No 7760 heading a train for Loughborough on the Great Central Railway. At the time, No 7760's main role on the GCR was to work a push-pull service between Rothley and Leicester North soon after this extension had been opened. *Malcolm Ranieri*

Above: Again on the Great Central Railway, ex-LMS 'Jubilee' No 5593 *Kolhapur* crosses Swithland Reservoir with a train for Rothley on 11 January 1992. *Malcolm Ranieri*

Right: Having departed Loughborough at 1pm, No 7029 *Clun Castle* passes Thurcaston with the Great Central Railway's 'Carillion' dining train on 26 January 1992. The locomotive had returned to service only a few months previously, having received a boiler overhaul at Loughborough shed. This scene has now changed with the completion of the Great Central's double track. *Andrew Bell*

Left: Early morning on No 5 road at Tyseley Locomotive Works, as ex-LNER 'A3' 4-6-2 No 4472 *Flying Scotsman* raises steam in preparation for the open day at Tyseley on 27 November 1992. *Robin Stewart-Smith*

Below left: Later in the day, *Flying Scotsman* stands round the turntable alongside Tyseley 'Castle' No 5080 *Defiant*, visiting ex-LMS Pacific No 46203 *Princess Margaret Rose* and ex-Great Western 'King' No 6024 *King Edward I. Robin Stewart-Smith*

Right: For a while GWR pannier No 7760 was painted in the London Transport livery which it carried in its last days of operation, so that it could once again run a series of passenger trains on LT, in company with No L99 from the Buckinghamshire Railway Society. It is seen here on the Great Central Railway, leaving Rothley with a demonstration ballast train for Loughborough. Ballast trains were precisely the type of traffic for which it was purchased from BR by LT. *Malcolm Ranieri*

Above: In the early 1990s *Clun Castle* was returned to service by the Great Central Railway and ran there for several years as well as visiting other preserved lines before returning to Tyseley in 1997. The locomotive is pictured between Woodthorpe and Quorn on the Great Central Railway with a train from Loughborough to Leicester North on 5 March 1994. *Andrew Bell*

Right: Following heavy repairs, ex-LMS 'Jubilee' No 5593 *Kolhapur* returned to service in 1990 on the Great Central Railway. Disguised as No 5552 *Silver Jubilee* (a pretence it maintained for several months), it is seen with the 9.30am to Leicester North on 12 June 1994. The locomotive subsequently toured various preserved railways before moving to Barrow Hill Roundhouse, where it is currently out of service awaiting a heavy repair and hopefully a return to the main line. *Andrew Bell*

Above: **Kolhapur** visited the East Lancashire Railway at Bury in August 1994. Here, approaching Burrs, it masquerades as long-lost sister No 45700 *Amethyst*, with a Fowler tender borrowed from a 'Crab'. *John East*

Right: On 3 September 1995 — 30 years to the day since the end of BR steam on the line — *Clun Castle*, bearing 'Cornishman' headboard and H32 reporting number, leaves Winchcombe with a southbound train on the Gloucestershire–Warwickshire Railway. *Malcolm Ranieri*

Left: Following restoration to main-line standard, No 7760 paid a brief visit to the South Devon Railway. Here, in a delightful setting, the locomotive nears Staverton with a demonstration freight on 11 October 1996. *Malcolm Ranieri*

Above: Victor, a powerful 0-6-0ST from Austin's Longbridge Works, was resident at Tyseley from 1995 until transfer to the Shackerstone Railway in 1997. It is shown giving brake-van rides on the demonstration line with Ian Hogarth as one of the footplate crew. *Michael Whitehouse*

Above: An unpublicised aspect of preservation at Tyseley has been the use of industrial shunting engines for their intended purpose. The collection features three designs: Avonside, Peckett and Hawthorn Leslie. Here, between shunting duties, Cadbury's Avonside 0-4-0T No 1 stands by the water column in August 1996. This engine was returned to Birmingham from Toddington with the help of owners the City of Birmingham and the Cadbury family. *Michael Whitehouse*

Right: No 7752 was repainted in BR black for photographic charters and spent some time on the Battlefield line on driving courses and scheduled services. It is seen at Shackerstone in April 1997. *Michael Whitehouse*

Above: A 'Hall' returns to steam at Tyseley shed. On 5 April 1998 Virgin Trains' Chris Tibbits performs the ceremony of unveiling the *Rood Ashton Hall* nameplate as No 4965 is recommissioned. Its true identity was discovered during the overhaul of what was hitherto believed to be No 4983 *Albert Hall*. The locomotive has been the mainstay of the 'Shakespeare Express' trains and has ventured up the Lickey Incline, conquered Shap, visited the South West and much more, delighting everyone with its classic lines set off by small (3,500gal) tender and authentic GWR livery. *Ian Hogarth*

Right: Newly recommissioned No 4965 *Rood Ashton Hall* stands alongside stalwart No 7029 *Clun Castle* at Tyseley on 5 April 1998. *Michael Whitehouse*

Left: Following a thorough restoration, 1945-built ex-GWR pannier No 9600, saved from the National Coal Board's Aberfan colliery, steams for the first time in nearly 30 years on 16 September 1998. The locomotive was completed in BR lined black, as applied to Old Oak Common shunting engines working the carriage sidings. It has since been on the main line many times, alongside fellow Tyseley engine No 7760. *Michael Whitehouse*

Above: 'Castle' No 5043 *Earl of Mount Edgcumbe* is the only engine in the Tyseley collection never to have steamed since preservation. This omission is about to be corrected, however, and the locomotive is shown here in Tyseley Locomotive Works undergoing a painstaking major overhaul to Railtrack Group standards, preparatory to joining the main-line fleet. *Michael Whitehouse*

Above: A timeless view. Following years of teamwork, a scene common in steam days is re-created. On 20 August 2000 No 4965 *Rood Ashton Hall* accelerates its train through Henley-in-Arden with the 4.50pm Stratford-upon-Avon–Birmingham Snow Hill 'Shakespeare Express', then in its second year of operation. *Andrew Bell*

Right: No 4936 *Kinlet Hall*, restored and maintained at Tyseley Locomotive Works, passes Tram Inn with a Stratford-upon-Avon–Newport train on 30 December 2000. *Andrew Bell*

Left: A summer's day, 5 August 2001, and No 4965 *Rood Ashton Hall* hauls the 4.50pm Stratford-upon-Avon–Birmingham 'Shakespeare Express'. *Malcolm Ranieri*

Above: Ex-GWR 2-6-2T No 5553 raises steam for the first time in over 40 years. This was the very last engine to leave the famous Barry scrapyard, on 31 January 1990, at which time it consisted of little more than frames, wheels, cylinders, axleboxes and boiler. Thus half the engine is new, completed at Tyseley Locomotive

Works on 28 June 2002. Here it stands in the late-evening sun, resplendent in BR lined green with 1956-style totem preparing for its first move at 8.40pm — a magic moment. *Michael Whitehouse*

Overleaf: Steam as it will be for a long time yet. No 7029 *Clun Castle* catches the last rays of the sun as it nears Quorn with the 4.00pm from Loughborough to Leicester North on 26 January 1992. *Hugh Ballantyne*